Charge into Reading

Decodable Reader
with literacy activities

blends

The Plum Plot
L Blends

Brooke Vitale • Mila Uvarova

CHARGE MOMMY
BOOKS
Riverside, CT

Copyright © 2023 Charge Mommy Books, LLC. All rights reserved.

No part of this book may be reproduced or transmitted in any form or by any means, electronic or mechanical, including photocopying, recording, or by any information storage and retrieval system, without written permission from the publisher.

For information address contact@chargemommybooks.com
or visit chargemommybooks.com

Library of Congress Control Number: 2023904018

Printed in China
ISBN 978-1-955947-34-3
10 9 8 7 6

Designed by Lindsay Broderick
Created in consultation with literacy specialist Marisa Ware, MSEd

Pam has a plot of land.

The plot has a pond.
The plot has plants.

Pam is glad.
She has a plan.

Pam plops the plums on a flat slab.

Pam splits the plums.
She flips the plums.
She pits the plums.

Pam plugs in a pot.
She slips the plums in the pot.

The plums get hot.
Pam spots clumps.

Pam blends the plums.
It is plum jam.

Pam slips the plums in a jug.
A glob of plum hits the slab.

Pam claps.
She had a blast.

Yum! Plums!

Let's Talk Literacy!

Read the sentence below. Then circle the picture that matches the sentence.

Pam blends the plums.

Let's Talk Literacy!

Each of the words below begins with an L blend. Sound out each word. Then draw a line from **each word** to its **matching picture**.

blimp   **clap**   **clip**   **flag**   **plus**   **slug**

Let's Talk Literacy!

Say the name of each picture below. Then circle the words that begin with an **L blend**.

Answers: flower, clock, block, plant, sloth

Let's Talk Literacy!

Read each word below. Then circle the pictures in each row that have names beginning with the same **initial consonant blend**.

blot

glad

slab

Answers: blimp, block / globe, glass / slug, sled, sloth

Let's Talk Literacy!

Say the name of each picture below. Then circle the correct **initial consonant blend** for each word.

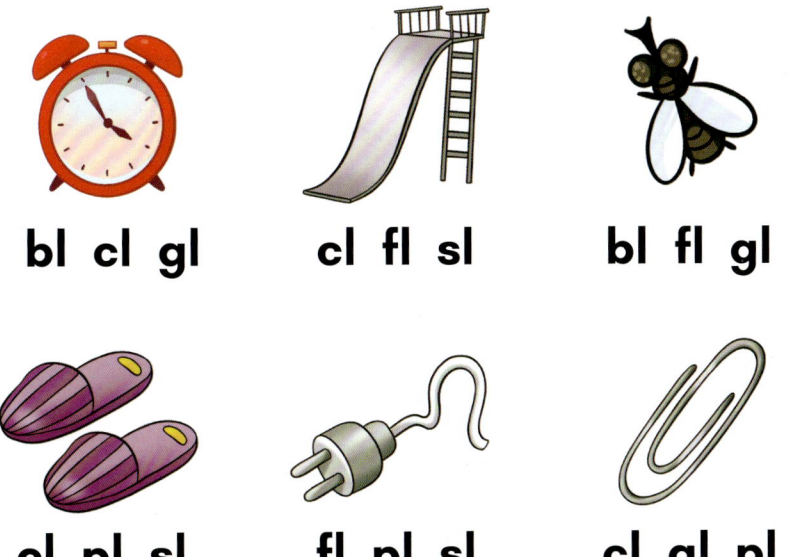

bl cl gl   **cl fl sl**   **bl fl gl**

cl pl sl   **fl pl sl**   **cl gl pl**

Answers: clock, slide, fly, slippers, plug, clip

Let's Talk Literacy!

Write the letters that form each picture word in the boxes below. Then draw a **scoop mark** under each consonant blend.

Answers: p-l-u-m / f-l-a-g / s-l-u-g

Let's Talk Literacy!

The name of each picture below begins with a different consonant blend. Sort the words in the **word bank** by putting them under the picture of the word that uses the **same consonant blend**.

| blot | glen | flat | slab |
| blab | slip | flip | glob |

Let's Talk Literacy!

Say the name of each picture below. Then write the word's **initial consonant blend** on the line below the picture. The first one has been done for you.

fl _____ _____ _____

 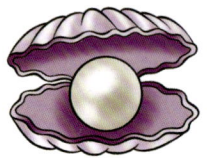  

_____ _____ _____ _____

Answers: fly, flower, glass, block, slide, clam, sloth, plane